MW00772964

Minoans

The Bronze Age Civilization
of Ancient Greece

Table of Contents

Introduction

"The last western society to worship female powers was Minoan Crete. And significantly, that fell and did not rise again." - Camille Paglia

The Minoans were the first advanced civilization in Europe. They appeared on Crete around 4,000 years ago and thrived for 1,500 years before mysteriously vanishing. It has never been fully explained what happened to them or who they were. Evidence shows they worshipped female powers but did so very differently to other civilizations. This book examines what this society might have been like.

This book is a complete description of the Minoan civilization and how it formed. It covers what type of government they had, who King Minos was, and how this society was so different from the rest. It discusses what their homes looked like and what they ate, as well as the artwork that they produced. Also covered are their trading habits and how they functioned as a society. The book also explains what happened to the Minoans, why they are important to us today, and why history must remember them.

The first chapter explains the Minoan civilization and how it formed. It covers what type of government they had and how this society was so different from others. You'll discover how this society was organized, what their cities looked like, and what was important to them. The second chapter covers their lifestyle, beginning with what they ate and how they dressed. It continues to cover what their homes were like and how people spent their time and how they were able to maintain control over such a large area of land is particularly intriguing.

The third chapter is about Minoan architecture, art, and trade. It talks about the famous Minoan palace at Knossos, which was perhaps the first-ever skyscraper. Their artwork and trade with other civilizations are also discussed. The fourth chapter is about King Minos and his possible role in the advancement of this civilization. It explains what he taught others about religion and even who may have built the famous labyrinth at Knossos.

The fifth chapter is about the history of the Minoans and how they fit into world history. It also explains why the Minoan civilization is important to us today, both good and bad. The sixth chapter discusses the decline of the Minoans. It explores the reasons for the decline of the Minoans and what happened to them. This book concludes by answering questions about their history and how important they were to our past. It explains how these people influenced the history of the world.

Chapter 1:

A Brief History of Minoa

The Minoan civilization flourished on the island of Crete from approximately 3000 BC to 1400 BC. It was a powerful and influential civilization that ruled the Mediterranean Sea. The Minoan Civilization is believed to have been founded by settlers from Asia Minor, although there are no written records or physical evidence which prove this theory definitively. There are, however, some signs which point to the fact that the Minoan civilization was, in fact, an Asian import. For instance, there are striking similarities between the sculptures and artwork of the ancient Minoan Civilization and that of ancient Anatolia. It is also known that spices such as mastic were imported from Asia Minor to Crete at this time.

How Was the Minoan Civilization Formed?

The Minoan civilization was formed through trade and commerce. The Minoans were great traders, shrewd businessmen, and fantastic sailors. The term "Minoan" comes from the Greek historian Thucydides who named this civilization after King Minos because of its architectural similarity to the palace at Knossos, the capital of Crete at that time. The Minoan civilization grew in power around 2000 BC, around the same time that Troy was flourishing. As they expanded into new lands, the Minoans established colonies in many different lands, and these settlements eventually became towns that were ruled by their local regencies.

Minoan Society

Minoan society was largely unstructured and egalitarian. There was no strong central government to speak of and the power of all nobles and princes were limited, due in part to a large class of merchants and traders. The Minoan Civilization functioned without any sort of monetary system. Instead, the people traded foodstuffs such as grains, fruit, and vegetables for other basic commodities such as tools and weapons.

Minoan society was notably peaceful. There is no evidence which points to the fact that the people ever participated in wars against one another. There were no forts or other military structures found in any of the ruins of Minoan cities. Also, no helmets have been unearthed throughout all of Crete, which also suggests that there was never a need to defend themselves from foreign attackers.

The Minoans even had an impact on the political power structures outside their civilization. They are widely considered to have invented the first system of democracy in recorded history. The Minoans were known to be enthusiastic proponents of democracy, and laws that restricted the power of elected officials over their constituents were written on tablets and displayed in public buildings such as temples and assembly halls.

The Minoan Civilization was also a very powerful maritime civilization. They had developed large fleets of ships that were used to travel to the Egyptian and Greek city-states. The Minoans were also known to trade with other civilizations in Mesopotamia, where they established lucrative trading routes to exchange goods such as spices, textiles, and metals for gold.

The Minoans' Residence

The Minoan Civilization thrived for many years in Crete. Archaeological evidence points to the fact that they also established numerous colonies throughout the Aegean islands. The Minoans did not develop a writing system until their encounter with ancient Greeks, which is why there are no written records of this civilization. Archaeological evidence points to the fact that this civilization probably began in around 5000 BC. The first major city was built around 2000 BC, and it thrived until 1450 BC. During this time, the Minoans established many colonies around the Aegean Sea. They traded with civilizations in Egypt and Mesopotamia while establishing contact with the early Greeks.

The Main Cities

The cities were mostly constructed on flattened land near-natural harbors or coastlines, much like most ancient Greek city-states. The Minoan civilization was also known for urban planning, which is why many of their cities are constructed on a grid-like pattern. This is different from the grouping system used by Egyptians, where buildings were constructed in large central complexes with other buildings clustered around them.

The main settlement was Knossos, which was most likely built in 1900 BC. In Minoan civilization, this city was the center of political activity. It contained ports, theaters, and large open plazas that were used for religious ceremonies. The city was probably not covered by any walls or other military structures. It is believed that the only reason the people of Knossos didn't think they needed to defend themselves was that they felt as though the island was not large enough for invaders to inhabit. They also probably thought that the island was too rocky for any invaders to construct a fort.

The next major city was Phaistos, which had been constructed from 1900-1700 BC on a fertile plain on the west coast of Crete. This city was built on a gridded street plan, and it may have housed as many as 15,000 people at its peak. This city contained paved streets and drainage systems that were built by the Minoans to handle water runoff. The last major settlement was Malia, who thrived between 1700-1450 BC. The island of Crete had many settlements during this period, but these three cities are notable because they still exist today.

Government and Hierarchy

The Minoan Civilization had a strong monarchy, but the kings could only rule with the help of a legislative body consisting of groups called "councils." These councils were made up of male citizens above the age of 18. Historians believe that this may have been a form of a democratic body because the people did have power over their government. The councils were responsible for writing laws and enforcing punishment for breaking them.

There was also a separate judicial system that consisted of judges who interpreted the laws, but historians are unsure about whether or not these judges were elected by citizens or appointed by kings. In addition to that role, other higher officials oversaw the government. The Minoans had a monarchical system of government that shared power with a legislative and judicial branch, according to the first investigation by the British School at Athens led by Sir Arthur Evans.

This society was organized in a very different way when compared to other civilizations around this period because it was more focused on creating an economic society rather than a large empire. They were able to achieve this because they relied on trade with others instead of conquest. This civilization is also notable for the fact that women seemed to have held equal rights to men in society, which was not common during this period. Women could own land and own businesses while also being able to represent themselves in court.

The Minoan culture was primarily focused on art and trade, which is reflected in the landscape of Crete. The island was filled with large open spaces that were probably used for farming. There are also many pieces of artwork known as "Minoan Villa" or "Minoan palaces" that show the wealth within the civilization. These villas were unique from other civilizations because they were not used as throne rooms for rulers but rather as living spaces for wealthy people.

The major cities also had unique layouts with large squares and grids to make movement easy.

Since Crete was mainly an agricultural society, most of their time was spent farming. As a result, several public spaces were constructed for the use of the common people.

What Was Important to the Minoans?

The people of this civilization placed a great deal of importance on religion and mythology. Their constructions were built to display religious symbols intended to honor their gods. The main god in Minoan mythology was the Great Goddess, who was believed to be responsible for creating everything. She is often shown in figurines and other artwork holding snakes, which are thought to represent male fertility.

Many of the structures found throughout Crete reflect this focus. The palace of Knossos is a good example. It was the center of political life during the Minoan civilization, and it contains many religious icons that can still be found there today. The organization of this society also reflected a great deal of importance on religion, as well as equity between genders. Many laws existed to prevent elected officials from gaining too much power and subjugating their constituents.

Minoa's Organization

For the most part, it is assumed that Minoan politics were organized like direct democracy. They conducted all major decisions as a group, with each citizen having an equal say in political matters. This society was also known for limiting the amount of power that elected officials had. They functioned as the leaders of the society but were not allowed to make decisions that would benefit them or their families.

It is also known that women had equal standing in society to men. This civilization was one of the first to recognize women's rights and never placed restrictions on their sexual freedom or practices. It was also extremely rare for Minoan women to be depicted in artwork holding objects that suggest they were housewives. Instead, they are often portrayed engaging in activities like sports or hunting, which was unusual during this period.

The Minoan civilization was ruled by King Minos, who lived in the grand palace at Knossos. It has been suggested that this society was extremely advanced in many ways, with some experts even calling it a utopia of its time. This idea is based on archaeological discoveries, which reveal sophisticated plumbing systems and artwork, which point to the fact that there were many different classes of citizens living together in this society. The Minoan civilization was ruled by King Minos, who lived in the grand palace at Knossos.

Surviving Texts

Surprisingly, there are many surviving texts and other literature regarding the Minoan civilization. While no official written records have been found, several different stories may have been passed down orally from one generation to the next. Despite the lack of extant texts, some scholars believe this society could have been literate.

The most important remaining Minoan records are the Old Palaces' texts. These documents were found in the Linear A tablets that were recovered from Knossos Palace. They provide information about leadership, crops, and taxes in the area during the period when this palace was occupied by King Minos. According to these documents, several aspects of Minoan politics were more hierarchical than previously believed. There are currently no surviving records that reveal anything about how the Minoans were governed or who sat on its ruling committee.

What Made Them Different from Other Civilizations?

The Minoan civilization is unique from many standpoints. Their religion was very different from the religions that their neighbors practiced. They were also unique in how they were able to maintain a large city with advanced infrastructure and trade resources. Additionally, it appears that this society maintained equality between genders, which was extremely unusual during this period.

Minoa's Religion

One of the biggest differences between Minoa and the other civilization in the Aegean was their religion. It was very different from what was practiced by their neighbors, and it had a large impact on how this society developed. One myth that has been passed down through oral tradition suggests that this region had some very strange weather for many years.

According to this story, several earthquakes shook the town, causing significant damage to the surrounding countryside. Many people died, and their livestock was destroyed, making it difficult for this civilization to sustain and grow its own food supply. With no alternative option for preserving a flourishing civilization, many inhabitants began to migrate away from the area toward neighboring Aegean islands.

The Minoan civilization was a unique and fascinating culture. While the government was a mystery, its economy and trade practices were very impressive. As mentioned before, they were also unique in how they maintained equality between genders, which made this society different from most others of its period. Even though no written records have been discovered to support this theory, many people still believe this region was a utopian civilization. One thing that everyone can agree on is that its legacy and influence on ancient Greek civilizations cannot be dismissed.

Chapter 2:

The Minoan Lifestyle

We know today that the Minoan Civilization flourished on the island of Crete between 2700 and 1450 BC. The period it existed in is referred to as the Bronze Age, which was a time spanning from 3000-1000 BC. However, before we dive into what daily life may have been like for these people many years ago, we must first revisit the history of this period.

The Bronze Age

Around the world, the Bronze Age is recognized as a time when humanity advanced through technological and artistic innovations. Scientists believe that these and other developments enabled people to become less nomadic and establish permanent settlements, which eventually evolved into towns and cities. This is one of the reasons why this time is frequently regarded as a transitional phase from a primitive to a more advanced human civilization, leading up to the Minoan Civilization and the Classical Period of ancient Greece.

There is evidence that people were migrating to Crete from the Greek mainland and other areas around the Mediterranean Sea, including Egypt and Turkey, around this time. This could be due to various factors, including crop failures and overcrowding, which occurred as the population increased. Evidence has also been found that suggests that people from these places were forcibly removed from their homelands. This evidence includes mass graves, where the bodies of young men and women who were killed before they had an opportunity to live in Crete have been discovered.

One of the fascinating facts about the Bronze Age is that it was during this period that writing was invented for the first time. We know that the Minoans did not invent writing because there is no proof of it, but we do know that they benefited from it and developed their own hieroglyphic system, which is still unknown to this day. The Phoenicians, a civilization that flourished in modern-day Lebanon, are accredited with inventing an early alphabet based on Egyptian hieroglyphs. This alphabet would go on to inspire this creation in ancient Greece, as well as a slew of others that would eventually become commonplace around the world.

The Minoan Way of Life

To understand what daily life was like for these people, we must first look at their hierarchy, which was very different from the society we live in today. Much of what is known about history comes from stories passed down through time about leaders and their subjects because they can give us insight into how these civilizations lived.

It is often noted that the Minoans had an advanced civilization for their period because people were allowed to worship their own deities, men and women were treated equally, and the end of life was not defined by religion. There was also evidence that at least the upper class engaged in some form of physical activity, as skeletons were discovered to have strong leg bones, implying that they were often running or jumping. This isn't to say that people wouldn't have had to work, but it does testify to just how important physical health was to them, and perhaps we can learn something from them today.

Apart from their buildings and artifacts, about which we know very little, there isn't much else we can say about this civilization with certainty. We do know that they had interaction with other civilizations surrounding the Mediterranean Sea, which is how they learned to write, but there is evidence that the people were far more advanced than we give them credit for even before this period. The discovery of the Phaistos Disc, an ancient tablet, is one such case.

The Phaistos Disc

This piece was discovered in modern-day Crete and is regarded to date back to around 1800 BCE. The Phaistos Disc is a mystery since an inscription on its reverse side is the only evidence we have as to what language was inscribed on it. What can we deduce about the Minoans from this? Unfortunately, because there are no other instances of this language, there isn't really much. Whatever the case may be, it still shows that the Minoans were more evolved than we give them credit for, considering there is no proof of what kind of civilization they were before this time.

Underwater Cities

Even more intriguing is the possibility of underwater cities that were previously thriving Minoan civilizations. This is because many artifacts have been found off the coast of Crete, especially near Santorini (which was destroyed by a volcanic eruption). In 1968, divers discovered a large, paved road that ran up to a harbor that was about 50 meters underwater, which led to the theory that these cities could still exist. This discovery is particularly intriguing because it indicated that there was once a civilization on Crete capable of constructing roads between major cities for trade and, most likely, general commerce.

These sites are often discovered by fishermen who bring artifacts to land for sale or trade. This has made it difficult to date these cities because no evidence preserves them, and we may very well be destroying other civilizations as we continue our search for more information. One such city which has yielded significant information about the

Minoan way of life is Zakros, which was excavated by Spyridon Marinatos.

Zakros Ruins

Marinatos began his excavation in 1939, and it did not take him long to discover that this site was possibly the capital for the city-state of Knossos. People were able to build homes with a full bathroom and kitchen, indicating that they were well-off enough to have a separate room for bathing, according to evidence found at this site. There was also evidence of a large palace nearby, which shows that this was the hub of its sort because no other structured settlement could be found in the area.

This excavation has given us a wealth of information about a society about which we still know very little, and it may help us learn more in the future. This is yet another part of our world that was formerly dominated by powerful civilizations that have since ceased to exist for reasons we may never understand. Hopefully, what has been discovered so far will give us enough insight into these people so that we can learn from them today.

We can figure out what they believed by looking at the history that has come down to us from this period because it often reflects their daily lives. There is evidence that these people believed in different gods, which provides us with insight into their perspective of the world. Since they couldn't distinguish between the natural world and their gods, their way of reasoning was very different from ours. Even though they were not religious, they had a spirituality that had a significant impact on how they lived their lives.

The Minoan Religion

There is some evidence that suggests that life came from the sea, which makes sense when you consider that it is where all living things first came from. This would explain the ritual that the Minoans used to honor their gods, which required them to pour water into a vase, then offer it as a sacrifice. They also seem to have believed in an afterlife, where they sent dead people off with parties and gifts because it was thought that these spirits could either wander around for 100 years or go to a better place.

The most popular of the Minoan gods was the Great Goddess, who embodied all of the aspects of her culture and society. Some people believed that she was the source (or mother) of everything, and even Zeus and other male gods were just manifestations of her power. This is why when someone wanted to give a name to the Minoan pantheon, they called them Zeus, Hera, and Poseidon, who were simply different aspects of the Great Goddess.

The male gods are believed to have been added on later in Crete's history because it was thought that having only a female god behind everything would make women more powerful than men, which is one reason why the Minoans were matrilineal. The arrival of the Mycenaeans also brought the Greek pantheon, which was very different from what existed in Crete, and this is probably when the introduction of Zeus, Poseidon, and Hades took place.

Another popular goddess in Minoan culture was Snake Goddess, who embodied wisdom, fertility, vegetation, and rebirth. The snake was important to the Minoans because it was believed that they could act as intermediaries between humans and their gods. This goddess was often depicted wearing a crown of snakes, holding one in her hand, or even surrounded by them. One of the most interesting goddesses is Mistress of the Labyrinth, who is associated with creation, birth, and death. The "labyrinth" she is connected to was thought to be a spiral design that symbolized the process of birth, and the snake was often associated with regeneration because it sheds its skin each year. The ancient Minoans were fascinated by this process and considered it to be very powerful, which may explain why this goddess is also associated with the snake.

Unfortunately for us, it is impossible to know exactly what they believed in because there are no written records that survive from this period. Instead, we have to rely on artifacts like the ones found at The Minoan Snake Goddess exhibit at The Archaeological Museum of Heraklion. This museum presents rare finds like gold rings with serpents, pendants, and small statues that were used to honor the Minoan Snake Goddess.

Not only do we know what they believed in, but we also know about their daily lives because of the artifacts that have been found. One great example of this is a cup from Phaistos (1700-1450 BC), which was found and is on display at The Archaeological

Museum of Heraklion. This cup, a deep bowl with concentric circles engraved on it, was used to stir wine with a stick as the swirling motion released its fragrances. They most likely drank their wine mixed with water because there was no way for them to make it pure.

The Minoans also traded with other civilizations in the eastern Mediterranean because they did not have much to offer. They were great sailors and could trade items like salt, cypress wood, cloth fabric, perfumed oil, dried fish, purple dye (which was very rare at this time), and gold which was abundant on Crete. This is probably why they believed that the island was protected by a bull-shaped god named after the Greek alphabet because they had to constantly fight off invaders.

Nowadays, Crete is known for its beaches, but it was formerly covered in forests of cypress trees, pines, oaks, and olive trees. It must have been breathtakingly beautiful and peaceful back then. Unfortunately, we will never be able to experience it for ourselves.

The Minoan civilization was peaceful, with women enjoying a high social status and not having to rely on men to look after them. During this time, art, architecture, spirituality, and trade all flourished, but it wasn't without its difficulties. They had great sailors who used the image of a bull, which they claimed came from an alphabetical god, to protect their ships. Women were held in high regard, there was no pantheon of gods, and artifacts representing their daily lives have been discovered. Unfortunately, it is impossible to know exactly what they believed in because there are no written records that survived from this period, but we do know a lot about their daily lives because of the artifacts that have been found.

Chapter 3:

Minoan Architecture, Art, and Trade

T he history of the Minoans is rich and diverse, including the lives of a plethora of kings and queens whose legacies have been lost to time. However, the legacy that has survived is that of the Minoan art, palaces, and culture. Minoan art reflects a brilliant and flourishing civilization that thrived for centuries before its mysterious end. In this chapter, we will explore Minoan art as well as the vast architecture across Crete.

The Minoan Culture

The Minoan culture grew out of the Neolithic times when people began cultivating fruit trees and farming vegetables in Crete. By 2700 BC, houses were built from stones placed on top of each other without mortar. These houses consisted of one or two rooms and had a hearth, water wells, and stone benches. Located on the island of Crete, which is one of five major islands in Greece, these early settlers grew wheat, barley, vines, and olives. There were also abundant herds of goats and sheep to provide milk products such as cheese and yogurt.

With such a good living, the Minoans began to build larger houses and by 2500 BC had turned them into whitewashed multi-roomed structures with paved floors and running water. There has been much debate over what caused the cultivation of wheat to begin in Crete. However, it is widely accepted that the reasons were related to trading and commerce. The island of Crete was located conveniently in the middle of the Mediterranean Sea, which allowed for traders to come and go easily, thus making it a hub of trade. It is also believed that Minoan sailors sailed south into the Atlantic Ocean, creating colonies along North Africa's coasts. As early as 4200 BC, Crete was trading with Egypt, importing goods such as wine and oil, and exporting goods like bronze.

When asked how they got their crops to grow so well in an area that experiences harsh winters, unlike the land where the grain was grown, archaeologists have three theories:

1. That Minoan farmers knew about using manure for fertilizer

2. The climate was much different at the time, and the island of Crete had more rain than it does today

3. There is a theory that has yet to be proven but states that the Cretan people were growing two crops of grain each year as opposed to one crop, which is normally done in such climates

As time passed, the Minoans developed more advanced agricultural techniques such as using plows pulled by oxen, horses, or even water buffalo. These methods of production led to an increased surplus which allowed for specialization in some regions. This new wealth encouraged the building of palaces and the creation of a middle class. The term "Middle Class" is used loosely as there was no such thing as money at the time.

The Minoan Art

Art was used as a tool to demonstrate wealth and power, as well as to tell stories. The island was inhabited by cavemen around 7000 BC, according to records. These people began carving stone into tools and weapons as they began to build an agrarian society. There is evidence that pottery production began in Crete around 2500 BC and that it was used for both storage and religious purposes. Female images were found on artifacts, which archaeologists believe to be representations of fertility. The snake goddess, an ivory statue from 1700 BC, is one such artifact. The Minoans worshipped women as objects capable of bringing life into the world, according to this illustration of a naked woman with snakes wrapped around her arms and held aloft in a threatening manner.

Around 1400 BC, the first forms of art were produced by the Minoans on a small scale and consisted mainly of ornamental designs. By 1300 BC, goods such as bowls and vases with floral motifs had been decorated with various colors, including red, yellow, brown, green, blue, or black. These items were not only used for decoration but also as a form of status. The more elaborate the artwork, the wealthier one was assumed to be.

Crete had extensive trade with most countries and societies around it, which led to cultural diffusion, and this influenced their art, as well as other aspects of their lives, such as architecture and religion. For example, around 1400 BC, the Minoans had started to use Egyptian forms in their art, such as the "Egyptian blue" color, which was a favorite of ancient Egyptians. This form of painting is called "fresco," meaning "fresh." Frescos consisted of applying paint onto wet plaster and peeling it off once it became dry. They were able to create these beautiful colors because of their use of minerals and metal oxides, such as pigments.

Famous Minoan Artwork

The Snake Goddess

This ivory statue is dated 1700 BC and was probably either a votive or funerary figure. It depicts a naked woman with snakes wrapped around her arms, holding them up as if she was threatening someone. They are believed to be symbolic of female fertility, as the snake was often associated with the Minoan goddess of nature and wild animals.

Bull Leapers

This piece is a fresco, which depicts people riding on the backs of bulls as they jump over a fence. Bull leapers were often displayed at religious ceremonies and have been dated to be from 1600 BC. The bull was sacred in Crete, and the belief was that if one entered a house, it must be given room to roam freely so as not to invoke the god of earthquakes, Poseidon.

The Prince of the Lilies

This piece depicts a male figure in blue and gold with hands upraised and wearing an elaborate headdress and short kilt. It is believed to be Minoan in origin, dated around 1600 BC. The lily was considered sacred in Crete and was used as a symbol of power and royalty, as well as a sign of fertility because it re-grows every year.

Male Figure, "The Prince"

This limestone figure dated around 1600 BC and was discovered in Malia. The figure holds a staff in his right hand and other objects which have been lost to time. He has a long braided beard and wears a cap decorated with a pattern of spirals. Minoan men did not wear capes or crowns, but they were often depicted wearing braided beards.

Pregnant Goddess

This stone figure is dated around 1800 BC and was found in Malia. The goddess lies on her back with her legs apart, showing that she is either deceased or about to give birth. She wears a crown with three-tiered spikes, which are believed to be symbols of the Minoan Triple Goddess, suggesting that she has given birth at least once before. The three-spiked crown is also seen in Egyptian art but is rarely depicted on pregnant figures.

Minoan Homes

Minoan homes were built with large open spaces to allow airflow and to keep them cool. The homes were built with tall columns, many doors and windows, and courtyards. There was usually the main room where the family would eat, sleep, and make crafts. Smaller rooms nearby may had been used as storage or for cooking purposes. In addition, many homes had a second floor. The civilization was very advanced for its time because it had several luxuries, such as running water and sewage systems. It is not known exactly how they made those devices functional, but it is thought that their extensive knowledge of mathematics helped them to devise ways to bring fresh water into the palace and remove waste.

Minoan Architecture

Crete was prominent for its advances in architecture. The Minoans were known for building cities on the coast and then digging into mountainsides to allow for access between different parts of the city. The first palaces and villas began appearing around 2000 BC and had more than one floor.

The Palace at Knossos

The earliest palace is believed to be Knossos, which was built around 1900 BC. The palace contained three major sections; the Central Courts, the West Court, and the North Entrance, each containing its own unique designs and purposes. The largest of these courts held grandiose festivals with feasts and bull-leaping events. They also held religious rituals for worshipping the gods, as well as law courts where cases would be tried.

The Palace at Phaistos

Phaistos was another palace built around 1800 BC and contained a large courtyard that was surrounded by columns on all sides. Three main staircases led to upper floors and a double throne room. It also contained storage chambers for holding goods such as oil, grain, and wine. Phaistos was destroyed by an earthquake in around 1600 BC, and the palace at Knossos took its place when it was rebuilt.

Saffron Walden

The Minoan civilization had great wealth due to their extensive trading of goods. They traded with the Egyptians for timber, metals, and precious stones. They also traded with Anatolian cities for silver, pottery, and luxury items such as gold. It is believed that saffron was first brought to Europe from Crete, which later became known as Saffron Walden.

Minoan Pottery

The Minoans were well known for their pottery, and they produced three types; White Painted (fine line patterns), Black (painted with red figures), and Red (with handle or spouted shapes). The pottery was created quickly on its route to the kiln and then extensively decorated. Glazes and natural colors such as purple, blue, and green appeared on the pottery after it was burned at a high temperature. The Minoans also made flower vases that had holes in them so that water could be poured out or through them.

Tools and Weapons

The Minoans did not have metal weapons or tools, so they used stone instead. Their flint was harder than the metals being produced in the Near East, which allowed for them to create sharper blades and arrowheads. The Minoans were one of the first civilizations to use bronze tools around 2600 BC, but this was still used for decorative purposes rather than as weapons or tools that could be used in war.

The Minoans had extensive knowledge of astronomy and were able to create accurate calendars. They used the stars and planets for navigation, timekeeping, and religious practices. They knew mathematics and were aware of astronomical phenomena, such as eclipses. They were able to predict lunar eclipses with an accuracy of within 5 hours.

The Minoans were also master mariners due to their advanced understanding of astronomy and navigation. It was around this time that many civilizations began building large ships for transport and war, but the Minoans had built large fleets before any other civilization. Crete was an early pioneer in shipbuilding thanks to their abundant forests, which allowed them to build the large and durable ships they needed for their extensive trading network.

The Minoans built ships with cedarwood, which was resistant to rotting and provided flexibility. The ships were also painted black on the inside but white or purple on the outside to help them stay cool by reflecting sunlight. They also had anchors that allowed for quick stops during trading missions, as well as steering oars that could be raised if they had engine power.

The Minoans built large ships called "bull boats" that were up to 50 meters long and 5 meters wide, which is twice the size of a modern fishing boat. They used these ships to transport cargo and passengers across open water and also for military purposes like transporting soldiers or supplies during battles. The Minoans also had smaller ships called "Pinisi," which were used for coastal trading and fishing.

The Minoan civilization was extremely advanced for their time and were an overall peaceful people. They had great wealth that allowed them to trade with other civilizations and obtain the resources they needed. They also made advancements in astronomy, mathematics, and pottery that benefited them as a society. The Minoans were pioneers of large shipbuilding during this period and were extremely skilled sailors. The Minoans' great wealth allowed them to trade with other civilizations, which provided them with raw materials, luxuries, and knowledge that they used for the betterment of their society.

Chapter 4:

King Minos

King Minos occupied the throne of Crete during its golden age and became known as the ruler who established the first sea trading empire. His palace at Knossos was lavishly decorated with works of art, many of which have survived to this day. These works of art tell the story of King Minos and his court. In this chapter, we will look at the Minoan sea trading empire, listen to some of the stories that were told about King Minos, and discover what everyday life was like in the palace of Knossos.

Family of Minos

King Minos, the firstborn son of King Zeus and Queen Europa, was born in Crete. Europa ascended to the throne after her father, Agenor, abdicated in favor of his eldest daughter. According to legend, each of the three kings, Zeus, Poseidon, and Hades, gave King Minos' mother a gift so that she could select which one she wanted for her child when he was born. She chose a stone wrapped in fabric that turned out to be gold. Therefore, he was born with golden hair.

Minos had four brothers; Rhadamanthys, Sarpedon, Rhadamanthus, and half-brother Deucalion. Minos and his four brothers grew up in the palace in Crete and were educated there. Minos took control of Crete after Europa's death, ensuring that he gained the sole rule of Crete. It is said that Minos prayed to Poseidon for a sign as to whether or not he would become ruler of Knossos. After the sign was given, he claimed the throne of Crete.

Ruler of the Minoans

While there may have been earlier rulers of the ancient Minoan civilization, King Minos is the one who became known as the founder of their sea trading empire. During his reign, there were many trade routes around and across the Mediterranean Sea. His people were skilled sailors and artisans who created their works of art as well as traded for more.

King Minos was said to be a wise ruler, but he also had a reputation for being harsh. To keep the peace on Crete, he often demanded recompense from those whom he believed had committed wrongdoings or desecrated any of the priests or temples. King Minos would often demand a hefty fine and return double what was taken as punishment for their offenses.

There were also times when he demanded an even worse punishment, such as branding the offender with a hot iron, cutting out his tongue, or hamstringing them. Nonetheless, it seems that all of the people gave him their respect because he was known for his fair judgments. It is said that King Minos had the finest stonemasons in all of Greece, working on his palace at Knossos. He also had excellent artisans who worked with gold, silver, bronze, cloth, and wood. The first written alphabet was created during King Minos' reign.

The Royal Court of Knossos

King Minos was married to Pasiphae, who he loved dearly. He had at least six known children with her, including Androgeus (a prince), Ariadne (Crete's first queen), Deucalion (who became ruler after King Minos died), Phaedra, Xenodice, and Glaucus.

It is said that King Minos had many women because he was known for taking wives who were widows or spinsters so he could have as many children as possible. The palace at Knossos became known for its extensive labyrinth with hundreds of rooms which included storerooms, passageways, dormitories, plumbing, and more.

The labyrinth was an underground maze that extended over 3 kilometers (1.8 miles) with many rooms that had different functions, including granaries, storerooms for oil, wine, grain, ivory objects, jewelry boxes filled with golden rings, and necklaces of gold beads. The cells were mostly built in the form of cubes and had no direct light. The walls were decorated with paintings that depicted people and animals, including bulls, dolphins, and sea monsters.

King Minos presided over his court at Knossos, where he wore gold crowns, bracelets on both arms, and a belt that was adorned with precious stones. He was often shown in frescoes as a tall, bearded man with broad shoulders and muscular arms. He also wore the traditional Minoan short-sleeved, or knee-length white belted garment called a kilt. His feet were usually bare except for a pair of bands on his ankles.

In some frescoes, King Minos is shown with his queen and courtiers offering gifts to the gods. He uses a gold cup and kneels before the seated deities, which included Zeus and Hera, as well as Poseidon, Apollo, Artemis, Dionysus, Athena, and Aphrodite.

King Minos' Court

His symbol was a double-headed axe, which was also seen on their coins. He was also fond of bulls and wore ornaments in the shape of this animal, which may have meant he had some association with the cult. Some historians believe that King Minos may have gained his position by marrying a queen who was also heir to the throne, while others believe that he came into power through warfare or by force.

It is said that the first year of his reign, King Minos had to go to war with one of Crete's neighbors, Nisus, because the ruler was jealous of King Minos' power. The Cretan king won this battle, but then he lost another battle shortly after against Lyctus because their ships were destroyed by a storm.

King Minos then went to war with Athens to protect his land, and he won this battle as well, even though the Athenians had built bigger ships. However, other sources state that King Minos' brother Rhadamanthys killed King Nisus, which would have made him heir to the throne, but some historians claim that King Minos killed Nisus himself. King Minos then had the support of his people, and many looked to him as a leader who would lead them to glory.

King Minos was considered one of the greatest rulers of Crete, but some legends claim that he was not a good husband, which led to his wife's suicide. One story says that Pasiphae was angry that King Minos left her alone when he went to war with Athens. She then had an affair with a white bull which resulted in the birth of the Minotaur.

King Minos was outraged when he found out about the affair, and Pasiphae threw herself off a cliff. Other legends say that King Minos killed his children because they conspired against him, but it is not known which children died. He then forced

Poseidon to send another white bull from the sea to placate the angry god.

King Minos married Pasiphae, a daughter of the sun god Helios and a mother goddess who may have been worshipped as a form of an earlier earth deity. He is also said to have had three sons named Androgeus, Glaucus, and Citrus, as well as two daughters named Xenodice and Phaedra.

King Minos is often depicted in art alongside his queen, the goddess Pasiphae, and one of his sons, Androgeus, who won various games throughout Greece. His other son is said to have angered him by killing a bull, which led to him being put on trial. It has been claimed that King Minos tried to sacrifice his son to the gods, but he managed to escape and was killed by a group of Athenian youths.

The Minoan Sea Empire

Minoan traders used the seas to set up an empire that was larger than any other contemporary trading system. Ships were transporting goods all around the Mediterranean and beyond by about 2000 BC. The earliest finds of Minoan ships are dated to 1900-1800 BC, but their seagoing capabilities were likely developed before this time.

King Minos was an accomplished seaman who often sailed across the Aegean Sea to trade with other city-states. His fleet of ships set sail from the port city of Knossos, which was built on an island in a harbor that opened into the Aegean Sea. King Minos' sea trading empire began when he fought for control of the trade routes with another ruler. The ruler who controlled these trade routes became very wealthy because merchants were forced to pay taxes whenever their ships sailed past them. King Minos' fleet of ships quickly defeated this ruler, and his trading empire became the dominant sea power in the Aegean Sea.

King Minos was not just concerned with trade, though. He also wanted to control other islands that were located near Crete so that he could have more resources at his disposal. The other island rulers did not like this, and they did their best to fight off the Minoan invasions. King Minos used his superior fleet of ships to invade many locations, and he became known for launching surprise attacks on other islands. The citizens of Crete managed to conquer many distant lands such as Egypt, Syria, Sicily, and Sardinia.

King Minos' Trading Empire

King Minos was known for establishing the first empire that ruled over islands and lands along sea trade routes. He was not the only ruler who had a fleet of ships, so it would be an exaggeration to say that he ruled all of the Aegean Sea. However, his fleet was probably the most powerful, and Minoan ships were the easiest to spot because of the emblem of a bull that was painted on their sails. Even after King Minos' death, his empire continued to grow, and the Cretan fleet became larger than ever.

Minoans used their ships for two different types of trade. One type of trade involved transporting local goods from one place to another within the Aegean Sea. The other type was known as long-distance trade, which involved sailing across the sea to deliver goods to places that were far away. Ships often headed towards Egypt, Syria, Greece, Italy, Cyprus, and Anatolia so they could bring back crops or acquire luxury items.

Most goods were transported by ship because it was the fastest way to get around. Cretan ships also brought back many goods from other lands. For example, Phoenician ships supplied Crete with high-quality timber in exchange for Minoan pottery and foodstuffs such as wine, oil, and grains. Cretan ships were not just used for transporting goods, though. They also played an important role in defense of King Minos' empire.

Religion in Minoan Crete

The Cretans worshipped many different types of gods and goddesses. Some of these deities were associated with nature, while others had dominion over aspects of human civilization. King Minos was seen as a divine ruler because he was related to certain important deities. According to legend, Zeus, the father of the gods who lived on Mount Olympus, had a child with Europa, a mortal woman. King Minos was the offspring of this union, and he ascended to the throne of Crete as a result of his mother's influence.

Zeus played an important role in protecting King Minos' empire because ships could not travel safely across the sea without his help. Cretan sailors were also not very skilled at navigating the waves, so Zeus sent Aegean winds that blew their ships across the sea. The route that sailors took to get from Crete to other lands was known as the "Etesian Winds" because they blew during summertime. Minoan ships could not sail against these winds, and they had no choice but to follow a certain path.

King Minos prayed to the god Poseidon, the ruler of the seas, for help when he sailed across the sea. The Cretans prayed to their gods in sanctuaries that were located all over their empire. These temples were filled with many different types of artifacts, and they served as a place where people could interact with divine entities. The most common type of artifact that was found there were stone sculptures called "labyrinthodonts" or "maze stones." These mysterious objects depicted people who were in the middle of complicated tasks.

The Cretans had many myths about King Minos too, and his connection with Zeus and Poseidon gave him an important place in their religious consciousness. However, it is not clear if the Cretans seriously practiced these beliefs or if they were just crafty ways of gaining power over others. They may have used religion to convince people that they would be protected if they submitted to King Minos' rule.

The Minoans were an advanced civilization that developed during the Bronze Age. They used their skills in pottery, metalworking, and construction to build a strong empire. King Minos was one of the most famous members of this society because he ruled Crete and built the legendary Labyrinth. He created one of the most powerful empires in ancient times, and he ruled over a great deal of land that spanned from modern-day Greece to Egypt. This empire collapsed much after King Minos' death, but it continued to grow even after his passing, so the Cretan influence was felt throughout the Mediterranean for many years after its leader's death.

Chapter 5:

The Decline of the Minoans

All civilizations go through a cycle of birth, growth, and death. Despite any presence they may have had in the past, all are destined to succumb to The Great Cycle. The Minoans are no exception. Once an empire that spanned much of the Aegean Sea millennia ago, their days are now rambunctious memories of what they once were.

A central trade hub, the Minoans traded their goods throughout the Aegean and Eastern Mediterranean regions. Along with being a wealthy kingdom on land, they were also powerful mariners traversing the oceans to bring back foreign crops, riches, metals, partisanship, and more trade. The civilization's prosperity came to an end with one simple disaster, a tsunami. The cause of this great catastrophe is unknown, but the results are all too evident to ignore.

The empire's land was flooded, and its cities were obliterated. For years nothing remained of their once-great civilization until the excavation by British archaeologist Arthur Evans began in 1900. Many significant discoveries were made during these excavations. However, what we know of the Minoans and their culture is still relatively little.

The Civilization's Existence

The Minoan civilization was the first great civilization of Europe. It is believed by most that they were a matriarchal society, and according to some, the first in history to respect women as equals. They worshiped primarily female deities and created art with scenes of nature and demigods. Along with their artistic and cultural advancements, they also developed and used written language and developed a very early form of writing called "Linear A."

The civilization's existence spans a long time frame, from c. 3000 - c. 1400 BCE. They were primarily a mercantile society with an ability to build and maintain great ships for trade and exploration. Their greatest achievements are the numerous palaces they built along with commanding locations from which they ruled from atop high peaks that overlook their cities below.

Their civilization was also composed of two distinct groups. The first were the commoners, who lived in houses made of mud-brick and limestone. These were the people whose lives were depicted on the walls of the palaces throughout Crete. Their general appearance seems quite humble to modern eyes. However, they were likely quite content with their lot in life. It is their lives that are depicted on the palace walls after all, so while they may have lived simple lives, their lives were no doubt filled with happiness and contentment.

The other group was made up of priests and rulers who lived lavishly within the confines of their palaces located throughout Crete. These people were far detached from the reality of their kingdom. The rulers lived in opulent environments made possible by tribute received through trade with other civilizations. The priests, on the other hand, performed ceremonies for the general populace and rulers alike.

The Minoan Legacy

Today, very little remains of the Minoans. Their great cities are in ruin, their history is largely forgotten outside of academics, and their legacy lives on only through Greek mythology. However, while it may be difficult for us to see where they went wrong so long ago, it's even more astounding seeing how far ahead of their time they were.

As it turns out, the Minoans were among the first civilizations to embrace literacy and standardized trade. They were also responsible for creating one of the world's first written constitutions (Crete's "First Law"). The people here lived under a system where all were equal under the law, with justice being served by their peers. This was a system so revered by the Greeks that the poet Homer referred to it in both *The Iliad* and *The Odyssey*.

The Minoans were also responsible for creating the first alphabets used throughout Greece. These would later be adopted by their invaders, the Mycenaeans, who would go on to play an instrumental role in the formation of Classical Greek civilization. It was their legacy that would become the foundation for our modern world.

The Minoans built many palaces that served as the center of their power. Many of these palaces have been restored today for visitors to see. The earliest palace was built in the Neolithic Era, followed by the first Palace Period c. 2000 BCE, which is at least partially attributed to king Minos I.

The prosperity of their society reached its zenith during the second Palace Period c. 1700-1450 BCE. During this time, the Minoans established themselves as a force to be reckoned with across the Aegean. They traded with civilizations as far away as Cyprus, Egypt, and Mesopotamia. In their backyard, they were involved in fierce maritime battles with Mycenaeans for control of trade routes and ports throughout the eastern Mediterranean.

Palace construction was revived with the third and final palace period c. 1700-1450 BCE. To expand their power base outside of Crete, Minoan sites were built across the Aegean Sea on islands such as Thera, Milos, Kythera, Lemnos, and Rhodes. It was from these locations that they engaged in trade and battle with other civilizations.

Despite the Minoans' extensive control of their island and its surrounding waters, they were no match for a tsunami that struck c. 1450 BCE. It is thought that an earthquake off the coast of Crete sent waves slamming into the coasts all around

Crete, destroying what had once been a thriving civilization. Without a navy to defend them, the Minoans were helpless before the waves, and their society was no more.

The palace at Knossos was destroyed during this time but may have been rebuilt for some time afterward until attacks by Mycenaean Greeks completely obliterated it around 1375 BCE. The city of Phaistos and its palace were also leveled around this time. The palaces of Zakros, Tylissos, and Malia have been more or less left alone since then as well.

The Evidence Left Behind

The Minoan civilization is an enigma that has puzzled historians for years because little evidence of their existence can be found outside the area they inhabited. No one from the Minoan Empire was known to have left behind any written history, nor did they ever leave behind a single artwork depicting their lifestyle and beliefs. What we do know about them comes from artifacts taken from excavated remains of palaces and other structures scattered throughout Crete. From these items, we learn that the Minoans were an artistic people with images depicting their everyday life. The subjects of their art were often the standard fare expected from ancient civilizations; war, hunting, agriculture, and ritual ceremonies.

The civilization's artwork is celebrated for its lack of fear associated with death; the motifs used are often gory but never show pain or suffering. Minoans loved nature, and the images they painted on their pottery portrayed that same love. The motifs usually depicted flowers like lilies and irises or trees such as palm trees and olive trees.

The decline of the Minoan civilization is still not well understood to this day. Waves devastated towns on Crete around 1450 BCE, and the palace at Knossos was burned down, but not without a fight, as one room shows signs that its occupants were prepared to defend it to the death. It's possible that the Mycenaean Greeks who were emerging at this time simply attacked the Minoans en masse and took their land. It has also been suggested that disease brought by refugee Mycenaean Greeks caused the demise of the Minoan civilization.

The Minoan Mark on History

The Minoan civilization was not just an ancient civilization but one that has left its mark on history by influencing future civilizations. The Minoans were the first known traders to bring goods from as far away as Egypt, Mesopotamia, and the Black Sea. They were also accredited with inventing the double-ax, or labrys, which became a symbol used by ancient civilizations such as the Greeks and Romans. The Minoans established a well-organized society that was extremely advanced for its time, and it's likely they were also responsible for developing the first known code of laws. Most importantly, however, is their contribution to our knowledge of ancient Greek culture and history.

The Minoan Empire was ruled by a powerful monarchy that controlled many other islands and cities in the Aegean Sea. This empire is believed to have been the earliest example of such an organized society, which would inspire civilizations such as Babylon and Greece. The Minoan civilization was also one of the first cultures where women were given more rights than in other ancient societies. Females could inherit property, own businesses, and serve in the government when they were allowed to become priestesses.

The Minoan civilization is one of history's greatest mysteries because so little evidence about their lives has survived through the years. What is known comes from artifacts discovered throughout Crete, but even these provide only a glimpse into what this great empire might have been like. The mystery of the Minoan civilization will likely never be solved because so much evidence has been lost or destroyed in earthquakes and tsunamis.

The Minoans did leave behind some clues about their civilization. The Knossos site alone has revealed evidence of more than 16,000 clay tablets containing Linear A script that is sometimes referred to as the "Minoan Rosetta Stone." This language, which is similar to ancient Greek and Etruscan writing, has so far remained undeciphered, but that hasn't stopped historians from piecing together a description of life on Crete during the Minoan civilization.

No matter their high standards of art and architecture or the fact that they left behind more clues about their lives than most ancient cultures, one thing is certain that the Minoans weren't afraid of death. Instead, they chose to adorn themselves with jewelry made in the shapes of snakes, lizards, and other reptiles, which would make anyone looking at them shudder in fear. These same people decorated their buildings with frescoes depicting bulls and dolphins. The fact that one civilization could be so different from another but still both be amazing is what makes studying history such a fascinating subject for many people.

The Role of Nature in Minoan Downfall

While there are many theories about the decline of the Minoan civilization, few scientists look to nature for an explanation. Earthquakes and tsunamis don't just come out of nowhere. The Earth is constantly in motion with plates shifting, building up pressure that can cause sudden catastrophic events when that pressure is finally released through a long period or with a violent earthquake.

These disasters may be proof of the ancient Greek myth about the Titan gods, with Zeus being the son who overthrew the Titans and claimed the rulership of Mount Olympus. Those who refused to serve him were sent into exile by Zeus, but they eventually found new homes on Earth, with Poseidon deciding to settle on the part of the island that would eventually be called Crete. While there's no scientific evidence to back this theory, it is a popular one with Minoan scholars because it could explain some of the earthquakes and tsunamis they experienced over time.

The earthquake that occurred around 1500 BC was probably caused by a nearby volcano erupting as the molten rock underneath the Earth's surface found a way to break through and spew out hot ash. This would have caused massive earthquakes that could have been felt all over the island, but probably not in nearby Greece or Anatolia because of how seismic waves work.

This was just one of many natural disasters that befell this civilization, which was already maturing as a culture, but still had a lot of growing up to do. They might have left of their own accord if they hadn't been forced out of their dwellings by earthquakes and tsunamis. They may have realized that living on a secluded island with natural disasters striking so frequently was simply too dangerous compared to what was going on in the rest of the world.

The End of the Minoan World

Even though they were extremely advanced for their time, it seems as though the Minoans never quite got over living in fear of nature and what it might do to them at any given moment. This is why there are no records of heroics from the people of Crete over this period because they were too busy dealing with the disasters that would strike them from time to time.

Minoan soldiers wore a lot of armor and had helmets which made it hard for them to see what was going on around them, but they didn't have many weapons at their disposal either, which is why there aren't any records of battles fought during this time. They would have had to pay tribute to the Egyptians who were in charge of their protection if they wanted an army, but this didn't happen until much later when the Minoans felt confident in their ability to defend themselves under any circumstances.

Even though Mount Ida was supposed to be one of the safest places on Crete because it was believed to be the birthplace of Zeus, this was not the case. The famous Knossos palace with its extensive plumbing system and air conditioning was one of the first buildings to be destroyed when a volcano erupted in 1500 BC.

This led many people on Crete to turn their attention towards religion because they no longer felt safe or secure under these conditions. They became very superstitious and started believing that the gods were punishing them for some of their actions. Others didn't care about what was going on around them, but they weren't exactly good people either, so it's hard to tell if they wanted to change their ways or not because of how self-centered they seemed to be.

The end of Minoan civilization probably occurred around this time when the Minoans finally realized Mount Ida was not big enough for all of them. They started moving south toward bigger mountains, but these were occupied by other people who wanted to take over what they had built over many years.

The Romans came in and took the entire island, but they did not stay long because the island was hard to control with all of the earthquakes and eruptions. They abandoned Crete but did establish a few ports around the island, which kept it alive through trading even though they weren't home to anyone who lived there then.

After all was said and done, the Minoan civilization vanished into the mists of time, despite being one of the most advanced civilizations in history at the time. It's difficult to say if they would have done anything differently if the eruption hadn't happened because it appears as if they were aware that their civilization was coming to an end when it did.

This is why many people are interested in finding out what happened to all of the people who lived in Crete, even though they were not as advanced as later civilizations. We can only imagine what could have happened if they had continued on their path of advancement, as they would have been the first civilization to establish a navy and expand into an empire if they had done that.

Even if this is a best-case scenario, it is intriguing to consider. If any artifacts are discovered around the island that could answer questions that have remained unanswered for centuries, perhaps we would learn more about them and their society one day. For the time being, all we can do is speculate on what may have happened if Mount Ida had not erupted when it did, allowing Crete to continue its advancement uninterrupted.

Conclusion

T he ancient Minoan civilization thrived on the island of Crete between 3000 and 1000 BCE, at which time it was destroyed by outside invaders. The word "Minoan" is derived from the mythic Cretan king Minos, who was said to have had a wondrous palace complex built in his name with advanced technology not possessed by others in ancient Greece. The Minoan civilization was destroyed long before the rise of Classical Greece, and its people were absorbed into Greek culture.

The word "Minoans" is used today to refer not just to the inhabitants of Crete but to a broad panoply of ancient cultures that flourished across Europe and Asia Minor from about 5500 BCE to about 500 BCE. The Bronze Age Minoans were sea trading people who traded with Egypt, the Middle East, and mainland Greece among other places. This trade was crucial in establishing Crete as an advanced civilization that had its unique art style, architecture, literature, and religious views.

The famously luxurious Minoan palace complexes consisted of spacious palaces furnished with water conduits, flush toilets, and other technologies not possessed by many civilizations until the modern era. There were also grand villas in the countryside decorated with wall paintings that depicted bulls leaping over obstacles during ritualized athletic contests, as well as frescoes showing women swimming in pools surrounded by lily pads. This last image is particularly curious, as it has been the source of much speculation that Minoan Crete was a matriarchal society where women were worshipped as goddesses.

There is little to no evidence that the Cretan religion had any female deities before the island was invaded and conquered by outside forces from Greece around 1400 BCE. However, the Minoans indeed worshipped a powerful "Earth Mother" figure, which may be interpreted as a form of mother goddess worship. There was also evidence discovered on the island of ritualistic bull-leaping, which was performed to honor male deities. This had led some to speculate that the island had dominant patriarchy before it was invaded, while others have claimed that the Minoans were a peaceful society with equal roles for both sexes.

The Minoans were one of the most advanced civilizations in history up to that point in time. They were not as powerful or influential as other civilizations which came after them because they had not yet established themselves on a global scale, but they were still very intelligent people who knew how to build things and create structures far beyond their time.

The eruption of Mount Ida changed all of that when it came to how advanced they were because it forced them to leave 1,000 years before many other civilizations rose and began to flourish. They were content with their island but didn't want to be pushed out because of the eruption or lose what they had created over the years, so they moved south and established a few ports along the way.

Many people try to find out more about the Minoan civilization because the little we know about them doesn't tell us much at all other than their skill as builders and how they were forced to flee from Mount Ida after it erupted. Some believe this was their fate because they had grown too arrogant and overconfident for their own good, but it's impossible to say what would have happened if things had gone differently.

Even though historians are constantly trying to learn more about the Minoan civilization, we now know that it has vanished into the mists of time. Nobody knows what happened to the people in that civilization or where they went. Some believe the Minoans perished after the eruption of Mount Ida, while others say they survived and thrived somewhere else where no one knew about their past.

References

Cartwright, M. (2018). Minoan Civilization. World History Encyclopedia. https://www.worldhistory. org/Minoan_Civilization/

Kris Hirst, K. (n.d.). What caused the rise and fall of the early Bronze Age Minoans? Thoughtco. Com. Retrieved from https://www.thoughtco.com/ minoans-bronze-age-civilization-171840

McLean, A. P. J. (n.d.). The Minoans. Lumenlearning.Com. Retrieved from https://courses.lumen-learning.com/atd-herkimer-westerncivilization/ chapter/the-minoans/

Minoan civilization. (2009, February 9). Timemaps. Com. https://www.timemaps.com/civilizations/ minoan-civilization/

No title. (n.d.). Study.Com. Retrieved from https:// study.com/academy/lesson/minoan-civiliza-tion-facts-map-timeline.html

Seiler, S. (n.d.). DNA analysis unearths origins of Minoans, the first major European civilization. Washington.Edu. Retrieved from https://www.washington.edu/news/2013/05/14/dna-analysis-unearths-origins-of-minoans-the-first-major-european-civilization/

The Editors of Encyclopedia Britannica. (2020). Minoan civilization. In Encyclopedia Britannica.

The Minoan civilization. (n.d.). Penfield.Edu. Retrieved from https://www.penfield.edu/webpages/jgiotto/onlinetextbook.cfm?subpage=1624570

Made in the USA
Monee, IL
15 July 2022